SUMMER
WRITING
JOURNAL
FOR BOYS

Copyright © 2022 Creative Path Publishing

Summer is a time for slowing down, playing outside, exploring nature, learning new things, reading more books, and making memories together. By writing in this journal each day, you will create a fun summer keepsake you can use to look back on all those treasured summer moments.

THIS JOURNAL INCLUDES:

- Sample Bucket List plus one to fill in yourself
- A Reading Challenge and Bingo to inspire you to read as many books as you can this summer
- A Nature Scavenger Hunt to complete while enjoying time spent outdoors
- A page to record activities to do when you're bored
- Pages to record summer memories
- 90 journal pages to record daily activities and answer a creative question or prompt to help you use your imagination

THERE IS NO RIGHT OR WRONG WAY TO FILL IN THIS JOURNAL.

Just have fun and enjoy your summer!

MY Awesome SUMMER

YEAR

THIS JOURNAL BELONGS TO:

I AM ------------------- YEARS OLD

THIS IS ME

SUMMER bucket list

- [ ] Have a picnic
- [ ] Build a sand castle
- [ ] Go to a library
- [ ] Play hide and seek
- [ ] Write & illustrate a book
- [ ] Have a water balloon fight
- [ ] Help cook dinner
- [ ] Go swimming
- [ ] Watch fireworks
- [ ] Roast marshmallows
- [ ] Ride a bike
- [ ] Read a book
- [ ] Run through sprinklers

- [ ] Take a hike
- [ ] Learn something new
- [ ] Make an obstacle course
- [ ] Build a fort
- [ ] Play a board game
- [ ] Have a dance party
- [ ] Make a treasure map
- [ ] Write a song or poem
- [ ] Make paper airplanes
- [ ] Family movie night
- [ ] Paint and hide rocks
- [ ] Learn a magic trick
- [ ] Watch a sunset

Summer Reading
CHALLENGE

How many books can you read this summer?
Color a sun each time you finish a book

Summer Reading Total _____

Summer Reading
BINGO

How many reading activities can you complete? Color a square as you finish each activity.

Read a book under a tree	Read a comic book	Read a mystery	Read with a flashlight	Read while eating a snack
Read to someone else	Read a poem	Read in pajamas	Read a book that makes you laugh	Write a book review
Read a book with a dog in it	Read a book about mythical creatures	Listen to an audiobook	Read a book based on a true story	Read a recipe
Read an adventure book	Read a book then watch the movie version	Build a reading fort	Draw a picture of a character from a book	Read in your bed
Read a picture book	Read a book with animals that talk	Read a fairytale	Read a book with a cat in it	Read a map
Read a menu	Read a book published the year you were born	Read a chapter book	Read a book and then make up a new ending	Read the first book of a series
Re-read a favorite book	Read a book that takes place in a city	Read a non fiction book	Read a book with food in the title	Read a book with a red cover

Nature Scavenger HUNT

How many can you find? Take your time!

- [ ] Something colorful
- [ ] A flower or petal
- [ ] Something bumpy
- [ ] A flat rock
- [ ] Something spiky
- [ ] Something that makes noise
- [ ] An insect
- [ ] Something rough
- [ ] Something round
- [ ] Two kinds of leaves
- [ ] Something with a hole in it
- [ ] Something scented
- [ ] Something triangle shaped

- [ ] Something thin
- [ ] A spider web
- [ ] A feather
- [ ] Something soft
- [ ] Something patterned
- [ ] A seed
- [ ] Something pretty
- [ ] A long and a short stick
- [ ] Something small
- [ ] A bird
- [ ] Litter (throw it away)
- [ ] A piece of bark
- [ ] Treasure (to you)

WHEN I'M BORED...

List 5 activities to do inside

1. _____
2. _____
3. _____
4. _____
5. _____

List 5 activities to do outside

1. _____
2. _____
3. _____
4. _____
5. _____

People I spent time with...

Places I went...

New things I tried or learned...

Movies I watched...

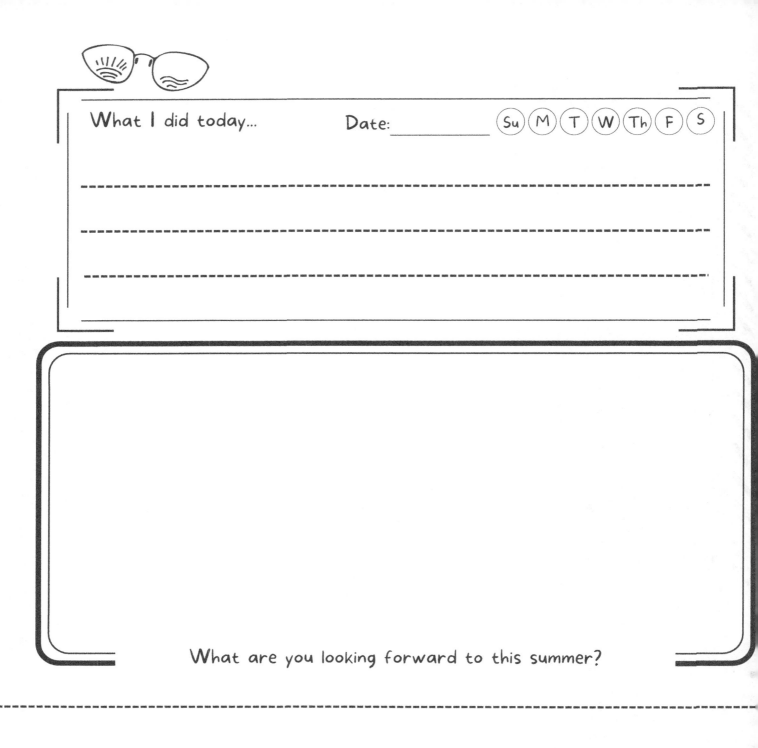

What I did today...   Date:_____   (Su)(M)(T)(W)(Th)(F)(S)

What are you looking forward to this summer?

What I did today...   Date: _____   Su M T W Th F S

‑‑

‑‑

‑‑

What was your favorite memory from school this year?

What I did today...   Date:_____   Su M T W Th F S

What would your perfect summer day be?

What I did today...   Date: _____   Su M T W Th F S

What is the most interesting thing you learned in school this year?

What I did today...　　　Date:＿＿＿＿＿　Su　M　T　W　Th　F　S

What would you like to learn this summer?

What I did today...   Date:_____   (Su)(M)(T)(W)(Th)(F)(S)

Write a silly story about what your teacher is going to do this summer.

What I did today...   Date: _____   (Su)(M)(T)(W)(Th)(F)(S)

Where is your favorite place to go in the summer?

What I did today...   Date: _____   (Su)(M)(T)(W)(Th)(F)(S)

Would you rather go to a beach or a water park? Why?

What I did today...   Date:_____   Su M T W Th F S

Describe how to make a sand castle.

What I did today...   Date: _____   Su M T W Th F S

How do you stay cool in the summer?

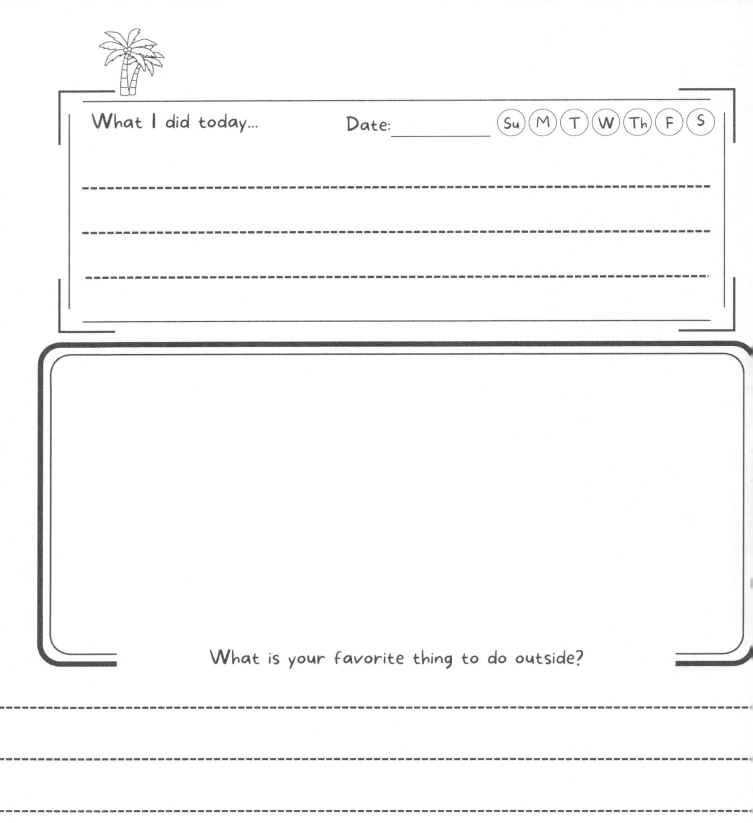

What I did today...   Date: _____   Su M T W Th F S

What is your favorite thing to do outside?

What I did today...   Date:_____   (Su)(M)(T)(W)(Th)(F)(S)

If you could have any summer job, what would it be? Why?

What I did today...   Date: _____   (Su)(M)(T)(W)(Th)(F)(S)

What is your favorite cold treat?

What I did today...   Date:_____   Su M T W Th F S

- -

- -

- -

Imagine you found a magic seashell. What magic power would it give you?

- -

- -

- -

- -

- -

What I did today...   Date:_____   (Su)(M)(T)(W)(Th)(F)(S)

You get to design a new amusement park ride. What is it like?

What I did today...   Date: _____   Su M T W Th F S

You've just learned how to fly an airplane. Where will you fly? Why?

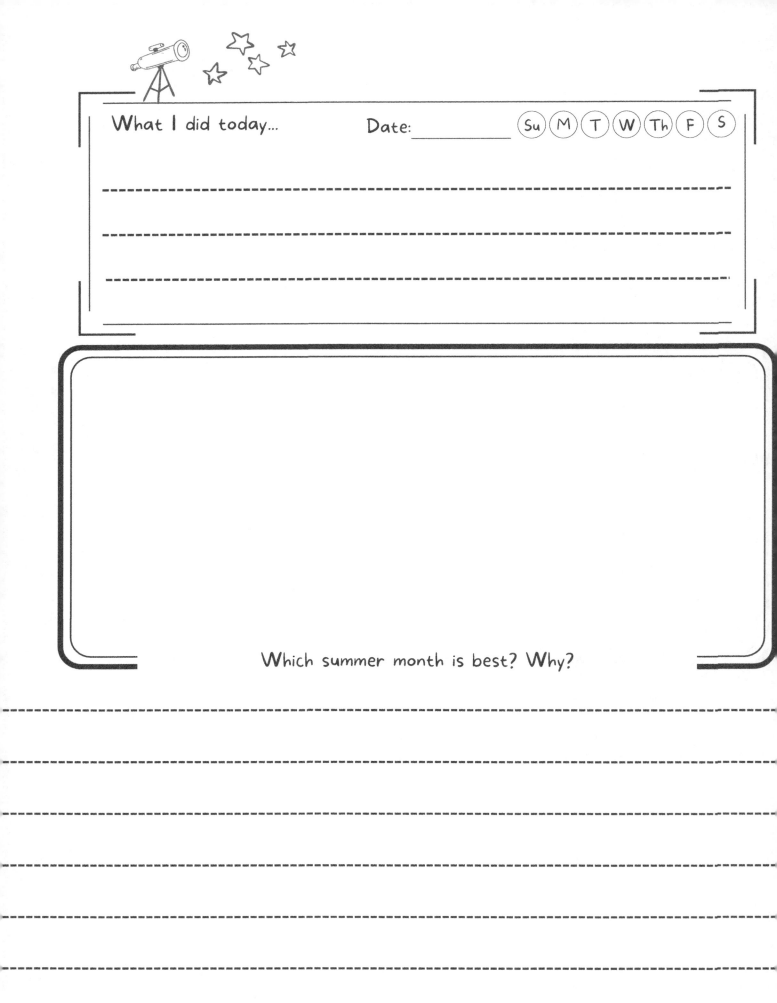

What I did today...   Date: _____   (Su)(M)(T)(W)(Th)(F)(S)

Which summer month is best? Why?

What I did today...   Date:_____    Su M T W Th F S

Describe a fun summer party. Who would you invite?

What I did today...   Date:_____   (Su)(M)(T)(W)(Th)(F)(S)

If you could go anywhere on vacation, where would you go?

What I did today...   Date:_____   (Su)(M)(T)(W)(Th)(F)(S)

What is your favorite summer food?

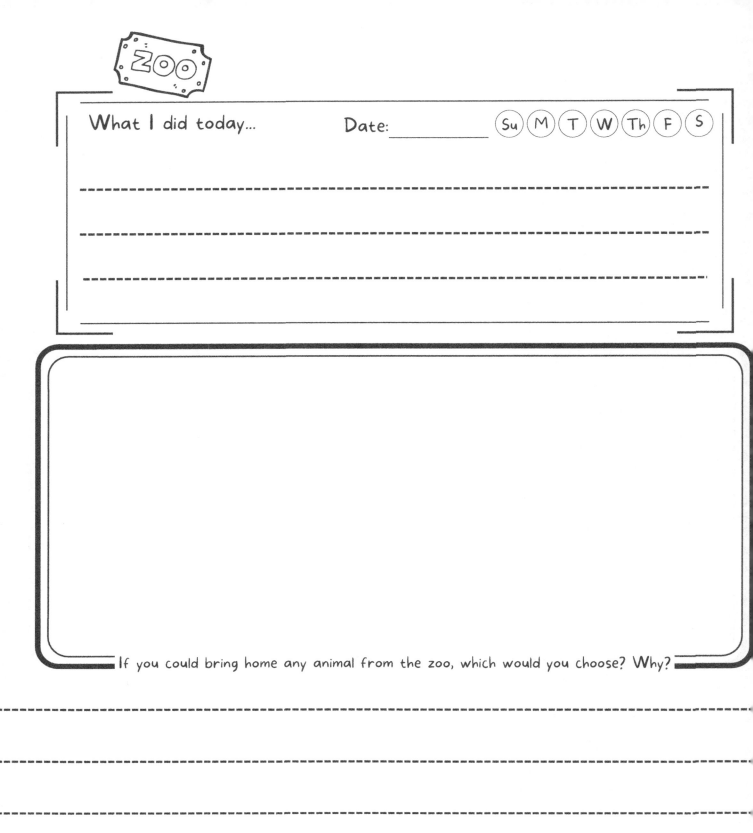

What I did today... Date: _____ Su M T W Th F S

If you could bring home any animal from the zoo, which would you choose? Why?

What I did today...   Date: _____   (Su)(M)(T)(W)(Th)(F)(S)

Would you rather go scuba diving or rock climbing? Why?

What I did today...   Date: _____   Su M T W Th F S

If it could rain food, which food would you choose?

What I did today...   Date: _____   (Su)(M)(T)(W)(Th)(F)(S)

- -

- -

- -

Name one thing you like about yourself. Why?

- -

- -

- -

- -

- -

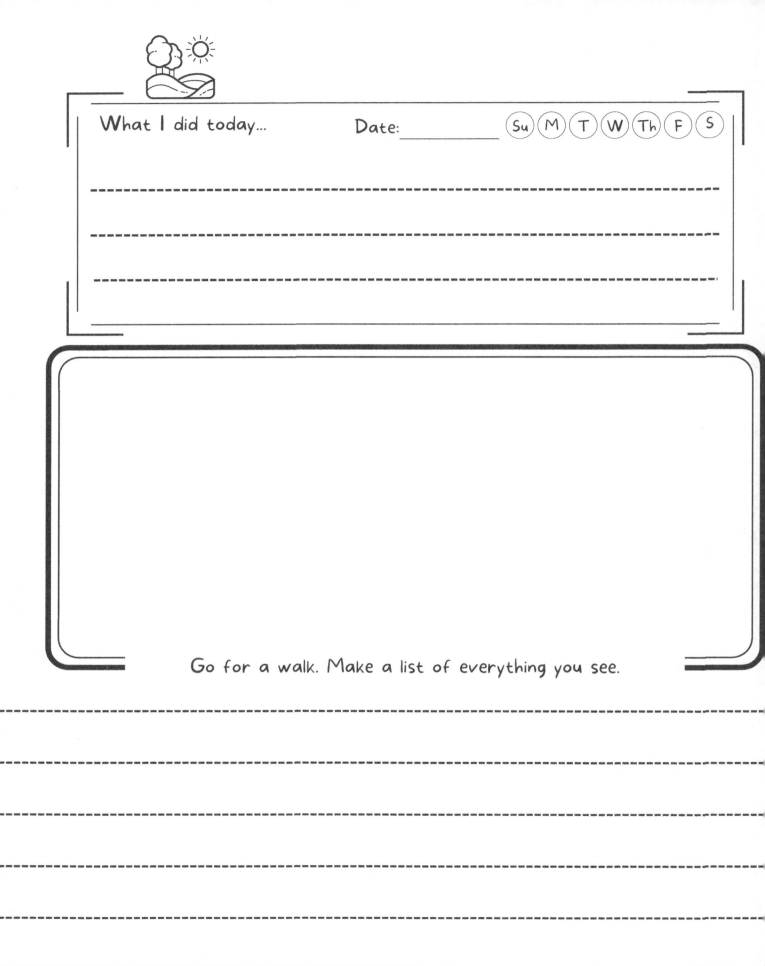

What I did today...   Date: _____   (Su)(M)(T)(W)(Th)(F)(S)

Go for a walk. Make a list of everything you see.

What I did today...   Date: _____   (Su)(M)(T)(W)(Th)(F)(S)

Do you like fireworks? Why or why not?

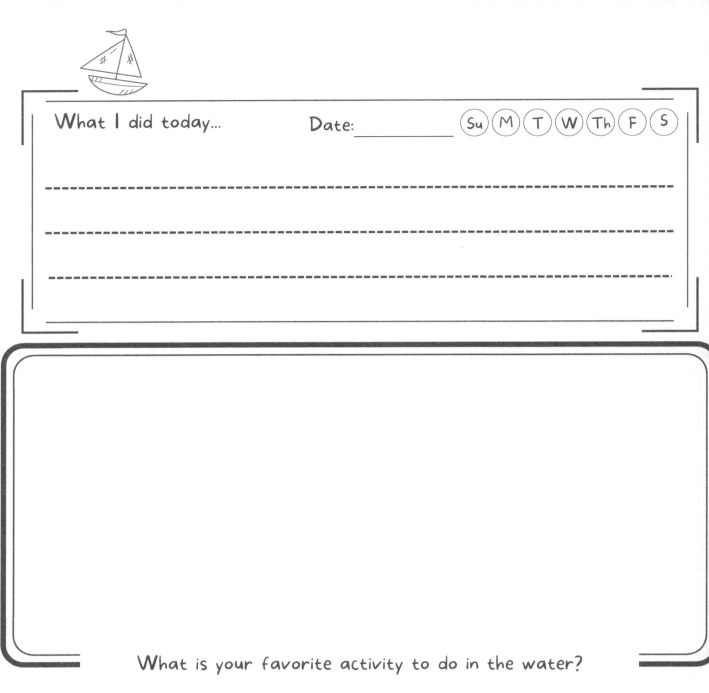

What I did today...   Date:_____   Su M T W Th F S

What is your favorite activity to do in the water?

What I did today...   Date:_____   (Su)(M)(T)(W)(Th)(F)(S)

Imagine your family is going on vacation in outer space. Describe your adventure.

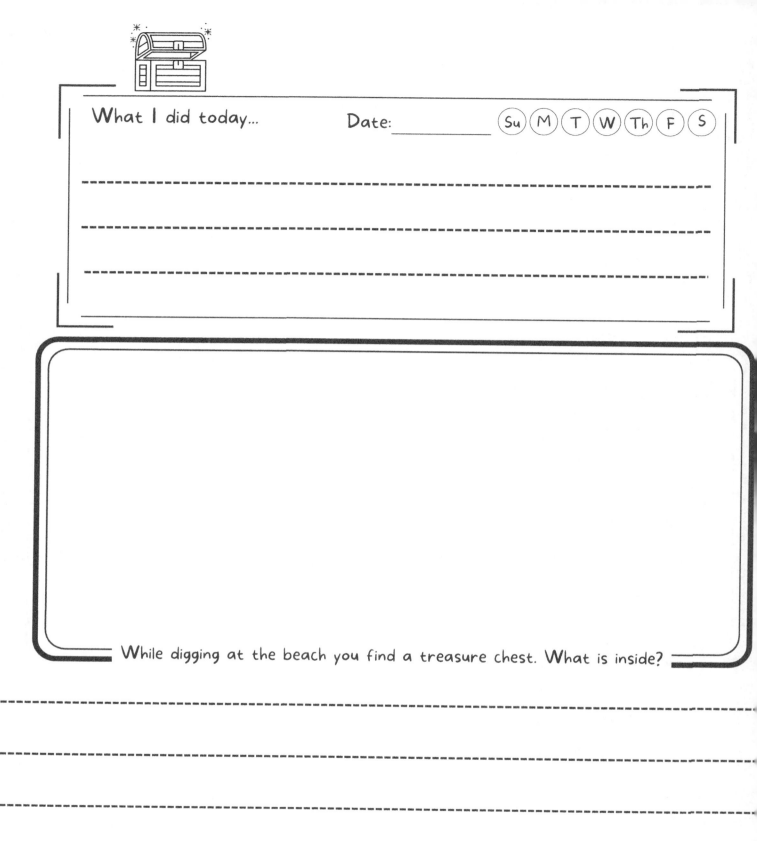

What I did today...   Date: _____   Su M T W Th F S

While digging at the beach you find a treasure chest. What is inside?

What I did today...   Date: _____   (Su)(M)(T)(W)(Th)(F)(S)

Describe how to make the perfect ice cream sundae.

What I did today...   Date:_____   Su M T W Th F S

Do you like winter or summer better? Why?

What I did today...   Date:_____   (Su)(M)(T)(W)(Th)(F)(S)

If you had one wish, what would it be?

What I did today...   Date:_____   (Su)(M)(T)(W)(Th)(F)(S)

If you were writing a travel guide for kids visiting your city,
which places should they visit?

What I did today...   Date:_____   (Su)(M)(T)(W)(Th)(F)(S)

Go on a scavenger hunt. Find an item for each color of the rainbow.

What I did today...   Date: _____   (Su)(M)(T)(W)(Th)(F)(S)

What would you need to pack to go camping?

What I did today...   Date:_____   Su M T W Th F S

You've discovered a new and rare sea creature. Describe it.

What I did today...   Date:_____   (Su)(M)(T)(W)(Th)(F)(S)

Draw a map of your room. What is your favorite thing in your room?

What I did today...   Date: _____   (Su)(M)(T)(W)(Th)(F)(S)

What is your favorite family summer tradition?

What I did today...   Date: _____   (Su)(M)(T)(W)(Th)(F)(S)

Describe one thing you could do to help someone today.

What I did today...　　　Date:_____　 Su M T W Th F S

- -

- -

- -

Imagine you are floating down a river on a raft. What do you see?

What I did today...   Date: _____   Su M T W Th F S

_____

_____

_____

You hear a scary noise while camping in the woods. What could it be?

_____

_____

_____

_____

_____

What I did today... Date:＿＿＿＿＿ (Su)(M)(T)(W)(Th)(F)(S)

If you had a tree that grew money, what would you do?

What I did today...　　　Date:＿＿＿＿＿＿＿　　Su　M　T　W　Th　F　S

Your family is going on a safari. Describe your adventure.

What I did today...   Date: _____   (Su)(M)(T)(W)(Th)(F)(S)

What food do you think is disgusting? Why?

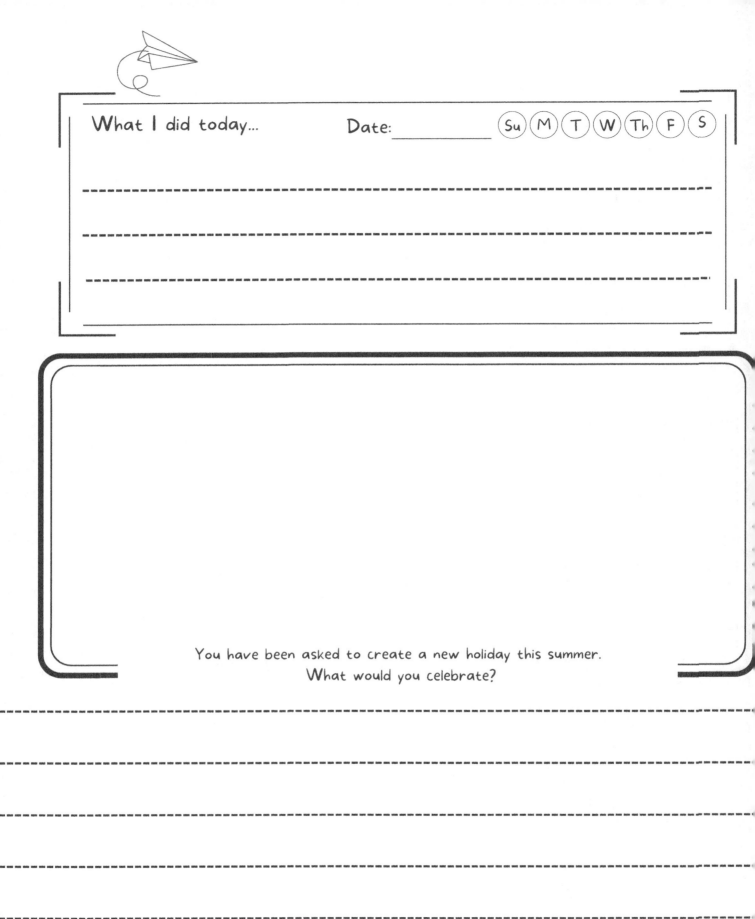

What I did today...   Date: _____   Su M T W Th F S

You have been asked to create a new holiday this summer.
What would you celebrate?

What I did today...   Date: _____   (Su)(M)(T)(W)(Th)(F)(S)

Describe your favorite toy.

What I did today...   Date:_____   (Su)(M)(T)(W)(Th)(F)(S)

If you could stay awake all night long, what would you do?

What I did today...   Date: _____   (Su)(M)(T)(W)(Th)(F)(S)

You accidentally swallowed some watermelon seeds, what happened next?

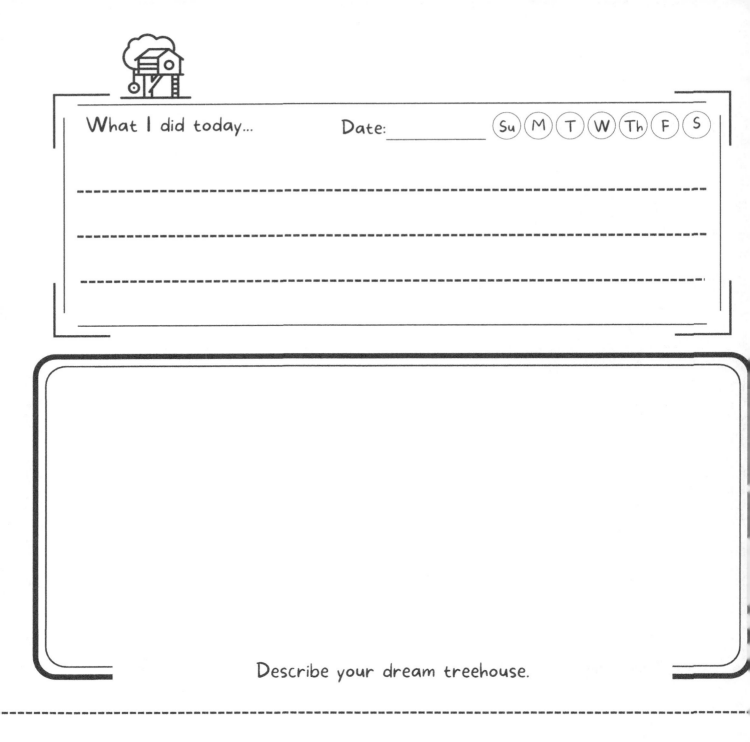

What I did today... Date: _____ (Su)(M)(T)(W)(Th)(F)(S)

Describe your dream treehouse.

What I did today...   Date:_____   (Su)(M)(T)(W)(Th)(F)(S)

What is your favorite thing to do at the beach?

What I did today...   Date:_____   (Su)(M)(T)(W)(Th)(F)(S)

What is your favorite thing about summer?

What I did today...   Date:_____   Su M T W Th F S

What if everything you touched turned to ice cream? what would you do?

What I did today...   Date:_____   (Su)(M)(T)(W)(Th)(F)(S)

What is your favorite thing to do indoors?

What I did today...　　　Date:_____　　(Su)(M)(T)(W)(Th)(F)(S)

Create an invention to make summertime even more fun.

What I did today...   Date:_____   Su M T W Th F S

Imagine you can breathe under water. What would you do?

What I did today...   Date: _____   (Su)(M)(T)(W)(Th)(F)(S)

You're at the beach and you find a message in a bottle. What does it say?

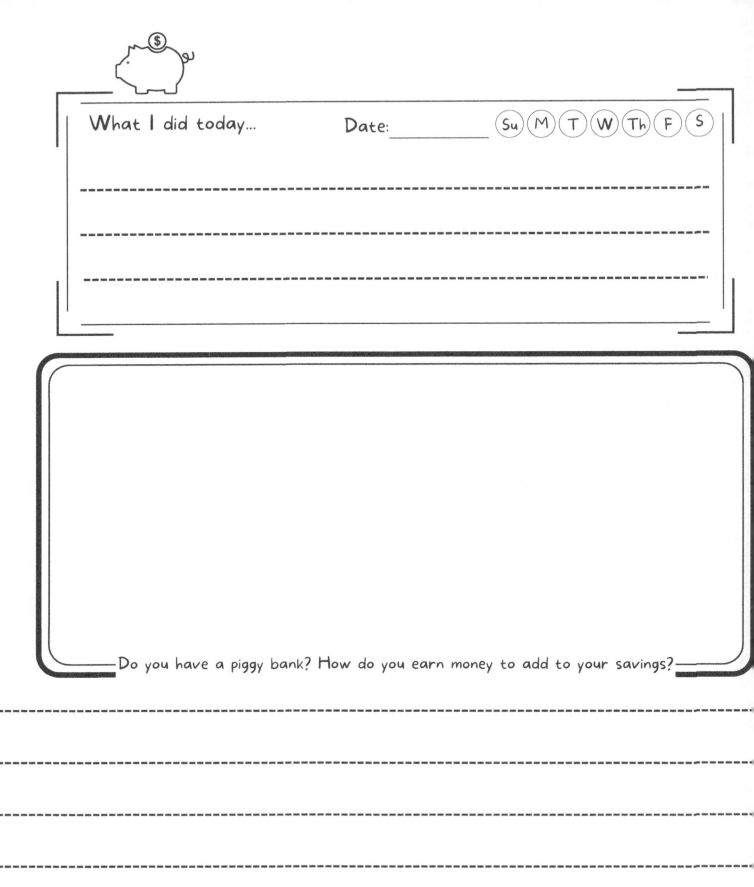

What I did today...   Date: _____   Su M T W Th F S

Do you have a piggy bank? How do you earn money to add to your savings?

What I did today...   Date: _____   (Su) (M) (T) (W) (Th) (F) (S)

Would you rather be able to fly or run extremely fast?

What I did today... Date: _____ (Su)(M)(T)(W)(Th)(F)(S)

Would you rather go swimming in the ocean or a pool? Why?

What I did today...   Date:_____    (Su) (M) (T) (W) (Th) (F) (S)

You discovered a new plant species. Describe the color, pattern and texture.

What I did today...   Date:_____   Su M T W Th F S

If you could live somewhere else for the entire summer where would you live?

What I did today...　　Date: _____　　Su　M　T　W　Th　F　S

You've invented a new flavor of ice cream. Describe it.

What I did today...   Date:_____   Su M T W Th F S

What would you do if you owned an island?

What I did today...   Date:_____   (Su)(M)(T)(W)(Th)(F)(S)

Look out your window and describe what you see?

What I did today...   Date: _____   (Su)(M)(T)(W)(Th)(F)(S)

Imagine what it would be like to live on a boat.

What I did today...   Date:_____   Su M T W Th F S

Imagine there is a blizzard in the middle of summer. What would you do?

1

What I did today...   Date: _____   (Su)(M)(T)(W)(Th)(F)(S)

You can only pack one item to bring on vacation with you.
What would you bring?

What I did today...   Date: _____   Su M T W Th F S

What are you grateful for today and why?

What I did today...   Date:_____   (Su)(M)(T)(W)(Th)(F)(S)

Describe your pet if you have one, or write about a pet you wish to own.

What I did today...   Date:_____   (Su)(M)(T)(W)(Th)(F)(S)

What is the first thing you think of when you hear the word green?

What I did today...

Date: _____   Su M T W Th F S

Describe the perfect summer camp.

What I did today...   Date:_____   (Su)(M)(T)(W)(Th)(F)(S)

Sit outside quietly for **5** minutes. Make a list of all the sounds you hear.

What I did today...   Date: _____   Su M T W Th F S

You are hiking through a forest when a tree starts talking to you.
What does it say?

What I did today...   Date:_____   (Su)(M)(T)(W)(Th)(F)(S)

Imagine you are opening a store for the summer.
What items would you sell?

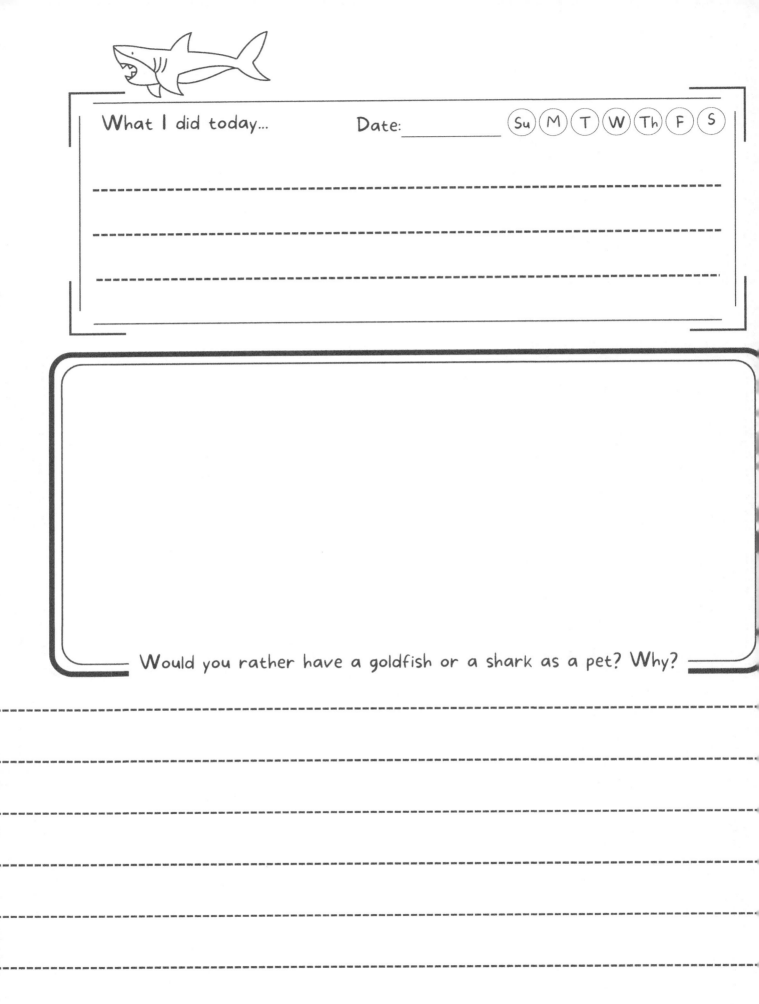

What I did today...   Date:_____   (Su)(M)(T)(W)(Th)(F)(S)

Would you rather have a goldfish or a shark as a pet? Why?

What I did today...   Date: _____   (Su)(M)(T)(W)(Th)(F)(S)

If you could only eat one thing all summer long, what would it be?

What I did today...   Date: _____   (Su) (M) (T) (W) (Th) (F) (S)

Do you think it would be fun to plant a garden? What would you grow?

What I did today...   Date: _____   (Su)(M)(T)(W)(Th)(F)(S)

What sport or activity would you like to learn?

What I did today...   Date: _____   (Su)(M)(T)(W)(Th)(F)(S)

Think of the last time you laughed really hard. What was so funny?

What I did today...   Date: _____   (Su)(M)(T)(W)(Th)(F)(S)

If you could drive a car, where would you drive to? Why?

What I did today... Date: _____ (Su)(M)(T)(W)(Th)(F)(S)

If you could learn to play any musical instrument,
which one would you choose? Why?

What I did today... Date:_____ Su M T W Th F S

You are given $1,000, but you can't spend it on yourself. What do you buy and why?

What I did today... Date: _____ (Su)(M)(T)(W)(Th)(F)(S)

What are 3 things you are good at?

What I did today...   Date:_____   Su M T W Th F S

What is your favorite summer fruit?

What I did today...   Date:_____   (Su)(M)(T)(W)(Th)(F)(S)

If you could be an animal for a day, which one would you choose? Why?

What I did today...   Date: _____   (Su)(M)(T)(W)(Th)(F)(S)

What would you do if summer lasted all year long?

What I did today...   Date: _____   (Su)(M)(T)(W)(Th)(F)(S)

What are you looking forward to this coming school year?

What I did today...   Date:_____   (Su)(M)(T)(W)(Th)(F)(S)

How do you prepare to go back to school?

What I did today...   Date: _____   (Su)(M)(T)(W)(Th)(F)(S)

What is the best way to celebrate the end of summer?

What I did today... Date:_____   (Su)(M)(T)(W)(Th)(F)(S)

What was your favorite memory this summer?

Made in the USA
Las Vegas, NV
18 June 2024